*Written by Pamela Hickman • Illustrated by Heather Collins*

# STARTING WITH NATURE

# Bird

## BOOK

Kids Can Press

First U.S. edition 2000

Published in Canada by          Published in the U.S. by
Kids Can Press Ltd.             Kids Can Press Ltd
29 Birch Avenue                 4500 Witmer Estates
Toronto, ON  M4V 1E2            Niagara Falls, NY  14305-1386

Edited by Trudee Romanek
Series editor: Laurie Wark
Designed by Blair Kerrigan/Glyphics
Printed in Hong Kong by Wing King Tong Company Limited

US 00  0 9 8 7 6 5 4 3 2 1
US PA 00  0 9 8 7 6 5 4 3 2 1

**Canadian Cataloguing in Publication Data**

Hickman, Pamela
    Starting with nature bird book

(Starting with nature series)
Includes index.
ISBN 1-55074-471-2 (bound)     ISBN 1-55074-810-6 (pbk.)

1. Birds — United States — Juvenile literature.
I. Collins, Heather. II Title. III. Series: Hickman, Pamela.
Starting with nature series.

QL682.H53 2000        j598'.0973        C99-932029-7

Kids Can Press is a Nelvana company

## Acknowledgments

Thanks to Valerie Hussey at Kids Can Press who suggested this series and, even better, asked me to write it. I'd like to thank my editor, Trudee Romanek, for her patience and amazing "text shrinking" abilities throughout the series. Thanks also to Blair Kerrigan for his great series design and to Heather Collins for bringing the books to life.

*For James,
Catherine and
Rebecca Hunter*
PH

# CONTENTS

# Meet a bird

What is your favorite bird? Maybe it is a heron, a chickadee or a woodpecker. The United States is home to all these birds and more. Whether you live in the city or the country, you will find plenty of birds to watch and listen to. In this book you will find out about birds from coast to coast and discover how you can become a bird-watcher and attract birds to your backyard or balcony. Start your bird-watching adventure by meeting the birds on these pages. These birds look very different from each other, but they have a lot in common.

Many birds migrate, or travel, long distances in search of food.

All birds have a beak, two wings, two legs and a tail.

All birds have feathers, and they are the only animals that have them.

## AMAZING BIRDS

America's smallest bird is the Calliope Hummingbird, which is found in the western mountains of Washington, Oregon, Idaho, California and Nevada. Its body is about as long as a stick of gum and it weighs less than some insects.

All birds lay eggs, and most birds build nests and take special care of their young.

# Beaks, feet and feathers

All birds have a beak, two feet and feathers, but why do they all look so different? Bird bodies are adapted to the different habitats they live in. Waterbirds may eat fish, while woodland birds eat seeds or insects. These birds have specially shaped beaks to help them eat their preferred foods. A bird's feet may be used for catching food or for getting around in its habitat. Feathers are important, too — they keep the bird warm and dry, they help it fly and they are specially colored to attract a mate or to hide the bird from predators or prey.

**Great Blue Heron**
Its large beak is perfect for spearing fish and frogs. The long, widely spread toes are designed for balance and for walking through shallow water.

**Red-breasted Merganser**
The sawtoothed edge on its beak holds on to fish Its feathers are waterproofed with natural oils. The webbed feet help it swim and dive.

## Ruby-throated Hummingbird
The straw-shaped beak fits easily into bell-shaped flowers and its long tongue laps up the sweet nectar.

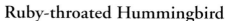

## AMAZING BIRDS
The Northern Shrike is a robin-sized songbird that feeds on small mammals and birds. Its beak is perfect for catching its prey, but the shrike's small feet are too weak to hold it. Instead, the shrike sticks its prey on large thorns in trees or shrubs, or on barbed wire, to hold the food while it is eating.

## Yellow Warbler
A pointed, tweezerlike beak is great for picking up insects.

## Snowy Owl
A strong, hooked beak is useful for carrying food and tearing it into pieces. The sharp claws, called talons, are designed to catch and kill small animals like lemmings and mice. In Alaska's ice and snow, white feathers make it easier to sneak up on prey.

## Pine Grosbeak (male)
The thick, strong beak is perfect for crunching and cracking seeds. Small feet are good for perching. Dull-colored feathers help the female hide while she sits on her nest. The male's red color helps it attract a mate.

# Bird families

A puffin lays only one egg each year, but a Ruffed Grouse may lay twelve eggs. All birds lay eggs, but they don't all lay the same number. Once the eggs are laid they must be kept warm, or incubated, until they hatch. Usually the female bird sits on the nest while the male hunts for food and feeds her. The female has an area of bare skin called a brood patch on her stomach. This bare patch lets the adult's warm body lay directly on the eggs to keep them warm. Incubation can take from 11 to 80 days, depending on the kind of bird.

Songbirds like Blue Jays are naked and helpless when they hatch. They have to be kept warm by the mother bird until their first, fluffy down feathers grow. The babies of ducks, geese and grouse, however, are born with feathers, and they can walk and feed themselves soon after they hatch.

tanager

Each baby bird has a sharp knob on its beak called an egg tooth. When hatching day arrives, this is used to break the shell open from the inside.

mallard

8

Baby birds are always hungry, and both parents work hard to find food for their young. Most land birds feed their young insects, but baby seabirds eat mashed up fish.

As the young birds grow, they soon become too big for the nest. Now it's time to leave home, or fledge. Even after a bird leaves the nest, its parents still feed it on the ground for a week or two while the fledgling learns to fly and look after itself.

herons

Do you have a bird in your pocket? The Bald Eagle appears on a U.S. coin – do you know which one?

Northern Gannet

Barn Swallow

Great Crested Flycatcher

Red-eyed Vireo

# Bird homes

If you were a mother bird, you would raise your family where the eggs and babies would be safe from danger. Some birds build nests in trees or shrubs, on the sides of buildings or cliffs, on the ground or even underground. Not all birds build nests, though. Razorbills lay their eggs on bare rock, while the Eastern Screech-owl uses an old woodpecker hole for its eggs. Here are some more amazing bird homes.

Common Murres breed in huge groups, or colonies, on cliffs along the west coast from Alaska to central California and off the east coast of Maine. Each female lays only one egg on the bare rock of a cliff ledge. The egg is pear-shaped so that if it rolls, it will move in a circle and won't fall off the ledge.

Eared Grebes build their nests on floating marsh plants in the shallow waters of prairie lakes and ponds. The nest is safe from land enemies like skunks, and the babies can easily step out of the nest for a swim.

Can you guess where Chimney Swifts nest? In chimneys, of course. These birds rest and nest on the walls inside chimneys. Swifts use their saliva to hold their shelflike nest of twigs together and to stick it onto the chimney wall.

The Baltimore Oriole weaves plant fibers, hair and twine into a deep, baglike nest. The nest hangs down from a high branch in a tree and even sways on windy days, like a cradle for baby birds.

## AMAZING BIRDS

Cowbirds don't build nests or look after their young. They lay their eggs in the nests of other birds and fly off, leaving a stranger to raise the baby cowbirds.

11

# Make a birdhouse

**M**ake a bird feel at home by building this simple birdhouse. You may get a family of sparrows, Tree Swallows, wrens or chickadees for neighbors.

**You'll need:**

a large (2-L) milk carton, rinsed out

scissors

2 nails

20 in. (50 cm) of thin wire

dry leaves or grasses

waterproof tape, such as packing or electrical tape

a hammer

1. Ask an adult to help you cut out a circle 1 1/2 in. (4 cm) wide, about 2 in. (5 cm) below the bend in the carton.

2. On the opposite side of the carton, use a nail to poke two holes. Place the top hole about one-third of the way down from the bend and the second hole about two-thirds of the way down.

**3.** Thread the wire through the top hole, down the carton on the inside and out of the bottom hole.

**4.** Put some dry leaves or grasses in the bottom of the carton to help attract birds.

**5.** Use waterproof tape to close the top of the milk carton tightly.

**6.** In the early spring, find a pole or tree in an open area. Hammer in your nails about 12 in. (30 cm) apart, one above the other. Wrap one end of the wire around each nail to hold the bird house firmly to the tree or pole.

**7.** Watch the birds nesting but remember not to get too close to the nest or to disturb the birds. If the birds don't use your house the first year, leave it up and try again next year.

## A helping hand

In early spring you can offer birds a helping hand by hanging nesting materials in the open on a tree or shrub. Try bits of string and yarn, hair from your hairbrush, small scraps of cloth or lint from the clean-out tray in the clothes dryer. Watch as the birds gather the supplies and fly off to weave their nests.

# Birds in winter

How do you stay warm during cold and snowy winters? You probably spend more time indoors and dress in extra layers of warm clothes when you go outside. Have you ever wondered how winter birds keep warm? Birds are experts at winter survival and they have taught us a lot about staying warm in winter.

Take a good look at birds in winter — do they sometimes look fatter than usual? On cold days, birds fluff up to trap air in their feathers. The air acts as insulation to keep the birds warm. The Gray Jay can puff up to almost three times its normal size in winter. When you wear a fluffy, down-filled jacket, you are wearing feathers, too — down is really tiny bird feathers. Some birds grow up to 1000 extra feathers in winter to stay warm — like putting on a winter coat. The ptarmigan even grows extra feathers on its toes! These feathers act like snowshoes, helping the bird to walk over the snow without sinking into it.

Huddling together in a group is a good way to stay warm. Chickadees gather in tree holes and starlings roost together in sheltered areas to share body heat.

The White-tailed Ptarmigan lives above the treeline in the Rocky Mountains and turns white in the winter to match the snow. This is called camouflage, and it helps the birds hide from their enemies. To keep from starving, ptarmigan change their diet in winter and eat buds and twigs instead of insects.

Ruffed Grouse survive cold winter nights by diving into snow banks to keep warm. The air trapped in the snow acts like insulation to keep the birds warm. Snow Buntings, Common Redpolls and other small birds also shelter under the snow where they are warm and hidden from enemies.

# Feed the birds

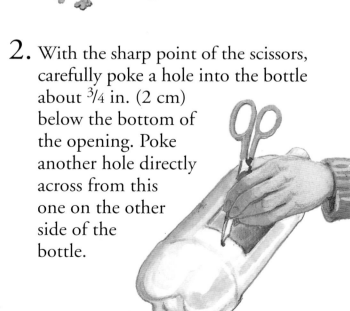

In the north, finding food in winter is just as important for birds as staying warm. In fact, the more birds eat, the easier it is for them to stay warm. That's because food gives birds the energy they need to heat their bodies. You can help your local birds by making a bird feeder and keeping it full of food all winter long.

**You'll need:**

a large (2-L) plastic soft-drink bottle, with lid

scissors

a stick (about 10 in. (25 cm) long and as thick as a pencil)

thin wire

birdseed

1. Rinse out the bottle. Ask an adult to cut an opening on one side of the bottle, about 2³/4 in. (7 cm) wide and 4 in. (10 cm) long. Make the opening toward the top half of the bottle.

2. With the sharp point of the scissors, carefully poke a hole into the bottle about ³/4 in. (2 cm) below the bottom of the opening. Poke another hole directly across from this one on the other side of the bottle.

**3.** Slide your stick into the two holes so that it is balanced in your feeder. Birds will use the stick as a perch.

**4.** Wrap one end of a piece of wire tightly around the neck of the bottle and tie the other end to the branch of a tree so your feeder hangs freely. Hang your feeder where you can watch it from a window and where you can easily reach it for refilling.

**5.** Fill the feeder up to the opening with birdseed. A mixture of corn, sunflower seeds, unsalted peanuts and millet will keep every bird happy.

## A summer bird feeder

Fruit-eating birds such as robins, waxwings and orioles will love this juicy, summertime feeder. Thread a wooden shish-kebab stick (available at grocery and kitchenware stores) with raisins, grapes, cherries, a partly peeled orange with both ends cut off, and any other fruits you have around. Tie a long piece of string or thin wire to each end of the stick and hang it from a tree branch or clothesline.

# Bird migration

As the days get shorter, many birds from Alaska and the northern states head south to find food. Insect and nectar-feeding birds like warblers and hummingbirds have nothing to eat in the winter, since the insects are either dead or hibernating, and flowers are gone, too. Waterbirds also migrate because their food and homes become covered with ice and snow.

Birds usually leave about the same time each year, in late summer or fall, and return each spring. Why do they come back? Birds return to the north because there is more food and space for nesting and less competition from other birds. Smaller birds, like warblers, usually migrate at night when they are safe from predators. Large birds, such as geese, travel during the day.

Not all migrating birds travel far. The Clark's Nutcracker simply leaves its Rocky Mountain home in the fall and heads down to the warmer valley for winter.

# Bird banding

How do scientists find out about where birds migrate to and what they do? Bird banders catch birds and attach a numbered band on a leg of each bird before letting it go. If the bird is caught again somewhere else, the number on the band will tell banders where and when it was banded. This information helps researchers learn many things about birds, including their migration patterns and how long they live.

If you see a wild bird with a band on its leg, try to read the band number with your binoculars. If you find a dead banded bird, ask an adult to help you remove the band. Write down the band number, what kind of bird it is (if you know), the date when you saw it (or found it) and where, and your name and address. Send the band and the information to: U.S. Fish and Wildlife Service, Bird-banding Laboratory, National Biological Services, Inventory and Monitoring, 12100 Beach Forest Rd., Laurel, Maryland 20708-4037. They will send you information on where and when the bird was banded, and who banded it.

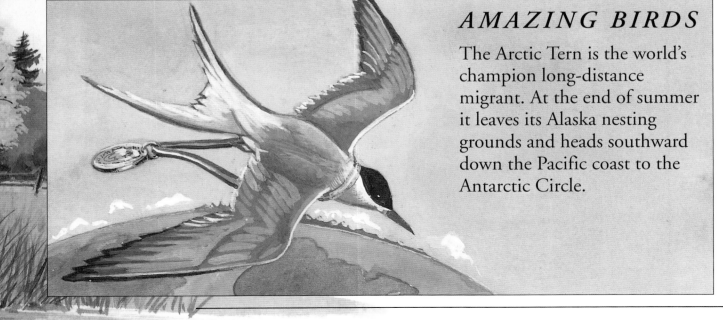

## *AMAZING BIRDS*

The Arctic Tern is the world's champion long-distance migrant. At the end of summer it leaves its Alaska nesting grounds and heads southward down the Pacific coast to the Antarctic Circle.

# Birdsongs

You may have heard a rooster crow at dawn, but have you listened to the choir of birds that sing as the sun is rising? Many birds start the morning with a song and continue singing off and on all day. They use songs to defend a breeding territory and to attract a mate. Birds also sing when they are angry, frightened or hungry.

In early spring, a male bird claims an area as his breeding territory where he and his mate will nest and raise their young. To keep other male birds away, he perches in high places such as treetops or rooftops, and sings loudly. The song means "no trespassing." When a female is nearby, the male changes his tune to attract a mate.

When you walk through the woods it's often hard to see the birds hidden among the leaves. You can hear their different songs, though, and with some practice, you'll begin to recognize a few birds by their voices. An easy way of remembering birdsongs is by thinking up words that fit the song's pattern. The clear whistle of the White-throated Sparrow sounds like the bird is saying "Old Sam Peabody, Peabody, Peabody." Other birds, such as the Killdeer, Eastern Phoebe, Black-capped Chickadee and Whippoorwill, sound as if they are singing their own names. Blue Jays, cowbirds and grackles sometimes sound like squeaky clotheslines, and the Gray Catbird actually sounds like a meowing cat.

*"Old Sam Peabody, Peabody, Peabody"*

*"chickadee-dee"*

*"meow"*

# Loon-y tunes

Try bird-watching with a tape recorder as well as binoculars. If you play a recording of a specific birdsong, such as a loon, outdoors, you may get a loon to call back or to fly into view. With some practice, you can start imitating birdsongs yourself. Repeat the songs you hear outdoors until they sound right and the birds start calling back.

# Beginner bird-watching

Wherever you are in America, you will find birds to watch. You will see them resting on telephone wires and trees, soaring overhead, swimming or wading in the water. With over 700 different kinds of birds in North America (excluding Mexico), you may wonder how to tell them apart. You can recognize birds by their shape, color, size, special body parts, markings and songs. If you see a bird with very long legs, you know that it is probably a wader or shorebird that feeds along the edge of the water.

This basic checklist will help you decide what general type of bird you are looking at. Then you can use a field guide to identify it.

size

shape

beaks

tails

color and markings

## Size

Is the bird small like a chickadee, medium-sized like a robin or as large as a pigeon?

## Shape

Does the bird have a plump body like a robin or is it slender like a swallow?

## Special Body Parts

What shape is the bird's beak?

Does the bird have long or short legs?

Is its tail long or short? What shape is it?

Are the bird's feet webbed, strongly hooked or small and weak?

Is there a crest on its head?

What shape are its wings?

## Color and Markings

What color is the bird?

Can you see spots or stripes on the bird's breast?

Is there an eye stripe, wing bars, tail stripe or other patch of color?

## Movement

What is the bird doing when you see it?

Is it swimming, diving or wading in water?

Is it hopping up a tree or climbing down head first?

Does it glide through the air, hover in one spot or fly up and down like a roller coaster?

## Location

What habitat, such as a forest, lake or meadow, is the bird in when you see it?

What part of the country is it in? Check the range maps in a field guide to find out what birds you can expect near you.

# Bird-watching tips

- Always have binoculars and a field guide handy.

- Take some birdseed in your pocket. Chickadees will often feed from your hand if you stand very still.

- Be as quiet as possible.

- Make a birdbath and bird feeder to attract birds to your yard.

- Keep a record of the birds that visit your feeder and birdbath and compare your lists each year.

# Seabirds

Some birds spend their lives out on the ocean and return to land to nest. The United States, including Alaska, has thousands of miles of coastline that provide homes for millions of seabirds.

Seabirds are well adapted to their special habitat. Their toes are webbed like flippers to help them swim. Puffins, murres and guillemots also use their short, narrow wings to swim underwater. To stay warm in the cold water, seabirds have a thick layer of short, fluffy down feathers next to their bodies. They also have a special oil gland at the base of their tails. The birds spread the oil on their feathers when they are preening to make them waterproof.

Most seabirds nest in huge groups called colonies. The birds crowd together in the best nesting areas near good food supplies, so more of them can survive. They are also safer nesting in colonies because there are many more eyes watching for enemies.

Murres are known as the penguins of the north. These black-and-white birds have short legs set far back on their bodies so they walk upright like penguins. Although both are expert swimmers, only murres can fly.

breeding

The Rhinocerous Auklet gets its name from the large knob that grows from the base of its beak during breeding season.

The Atlantic Puffin is sometimes called a sea parrot because of its large, colorful, striped beak. After breeding season is over, its beak gets smaller and duller.

# Prairie birds

You may be used to seeing birds up in trees, but there are lots of birds in the open prairies, too. The grasslands and prairie sloughs (shallow, marshy ponds) are perfect habitats for many different birds. In fact, over half the ducks born in North America start their life in small prairie wetlands. Many of the birds in the prairie grasslands are sandy-colored or brown, blending in well with the dry prairie. Even their eggs are light colored with brown spots for camouflage.

**Burrowing Owl**
Small, long-legged Burrowing Owls live in open grasslands from the plains states west to California. Their nests are built in underground burrows left by small prairie mammals. Unlike most other owls, Burrowing Owls are active during the day and night.

**Sharp-tailed Grouse**
Each spring, Sharp-tailed Grouse gather on their special prairie dancing grounds, where the males put on a great display of foot stomping and noise making to attract a mate. The males inflate their purple neck pouches like small balloons and make a low booming sound to attract females.

## Swainson's Hawk

If you see a large, brown-and-white hawk perched on a roadside fence, it is probably a Swainson's Hawk — one of the most common hawks on the Great Plains. It feeds on the mice, gophers and large grasshoppers that live in the grasslands.

### AMAZING BIRDS

The Prairie Warbler is not found in the prairies. It breeds in dry, shrubby areas in the eastern U.S.

## Marbled Godwit

You can tell that the Marbled Godwit is a shorebird by its long legs and long, slender beak. This large bird comes to the prairies in summer to breed in the grasslands and feed at the edges of sloughs and lakes.

## Ruddy Duck

This small diving duck breeds mainly in the grasslands, especially in lakes, ponds and marshes. It weaves marsh plants into a nest hidden among the reeds and cattails.

# Birds and you

**T**ry to imagine a world without birds. You would miss their songs and pretty colors, but birds add much more to our world than that.

Birds are an important part of the wildlife food chain. Foxes, weasels, coyotes, mink, lynx, snakes and snapping turtles are some of the predators that feed on birds. Birds' eggs are also eaten by many animals such as raccoons and skunks. All these creatures, and many more, depend on birds for survival.

Plants depend on birds, too. Flowers make seeds, and then more flowers, when they are pollinated. Hummingbirds pollinate flowers when they visit them to feed on the nectar. Fruit-eating birds such as robins are great for spreading seeds around. Since these birds can't digest the seeds, they come out in the birds' droppings, often a long way from where the fruit was picked.

Birds are very important to farmers because they eat millions of insect pests and weed seeds that could damage crops. They also eat mosquitoes, blackflies and other nuisance insects.

# America's state birds

Each state has chosen a bird to represent the state. Some birds have been chosen by more than one state. For instance, the Cardinal represents seven different states. Check out the list below and find your state bird.

| | |
|---|---|
| Alabama | Yellowhammer |
| Alaska | Willow Ptarmigan |
| Arizona | Cactus Wren |
| Arkansas | Mockingbird |
| California | California Valley Quail |
| Colorado | Lark Bunting |
| Connecticut | American Robin |
| Delaware | Blue Hen's Chicken |
| Florida | Mockingbird |
| Georgia | Brown Thrasher |
| Hawaii | Nene (Hawaiian goose) |
| Idaho | Mountain Bluebird |
| Illinois | Cardinal |
| Indiana | Cardinal |
| Iowa | Eastern Goldfinch |
| Kansas | Western Meadowlark |
| Kentucky | Cardinal |
| Louisiana | Eastern Brown Pelican |
| Maine | Chickadee |
| Maryland | Baltimore Oriole |
| Massachusetts | Chickadee |
| Michigan | Robin |
| Minnesota | Common Loon |
| Mississippi | Mockingbird |
| Missouri | Bluebird |
| Montana | Western Meadowlark |
| Nebraska | Western Meadowlark |
| Nevada | Mountain Bluebird |
| New Hampshire | Purple Finch |
| New Jersey | Goldfinch |
| New Mexico | Roadrunner |
| New York | Bluebird |
| North Carolina | Cardinal |
| North Dakota | Western Meadowlark |
| Ohio | Cardinal |
| Oklahoma | Scissor-tailed Flycatcher |
| Oregon | Western Meadowlark |
| Pennsylvania | Ruffed Grouse |
| Rhode Island | Rhode Island Red |
| South Carolina | Carolina Wren |
| South Dakota | Chinese Ring-necked Pheasant |
| Tennessee | Mockingbird |
| Texas | Mockingbird |
| Utah | Seagull |
| Vermont | Hermit Thrush |
| Virginia | Cardinal |
| Washington | Goldfinch |
| West Virginia | Cardinal |
| Wisconsin | Robin |
| Wyoming | Meadowlark |

# Endangered birds

Imagine if a bulldozer knocked down your home. You'd have to find somewhere else to live. Many birds across the country have their homes destroyed each day as forests are cut down, wetlands are drained and grasslands are ploughed under for farms, roads and subdivisions. Oil spills and other pollution is another problem that threatens birds and their habitats. It's not always possible for birds to find new homes when theirs are destroyed. Loss of their habitat is endangering some birds.

When a species is endangered it means that something is killing it. If it isn't helped, all the birds of that species may die. When this happens, the species is extinct and is found nowhere in the world. The Labrador Duck, the Carolina Parakeet and the Passenger Pigeon are examples of extinct U.S. birds.

Labrador Duck

## Endangered birds

These are some birds listed as endangered in the U.S.

| | Bird | Range in U.S. |
|---|---|---|
| 1 | Whooping Crane | Rocky Mountains east to Carolinas |
| 2 | Eskimo Curlew | east coast in fall, Great Plains in spring |
| 3 | Peregrine Falcon | all U.S. |
| 4 | Piping Plover | Great Lakes, Virginia, Atlantic/Gulf coasts, Northern Great Plains |
| 5 | Kirtland's Warbler | North Central Michigan |
| 6 | Brown Pelican | Carolina–Texas to west coast |
| 7 | California Condor | Oregon, California and Baja California |
| 8 | Thick-billed Parrot | Arizona, New Mexico |
| 9 | Red-cockaded Woodpecker | south-central and south-eastern U.S. |
| 10 | Everglade Snail Kite | Florida |
| 11 | Attwater's Prairie Chicken | Texas |
| 12 | Bachman's Warbler | south-eastern U.S. |
| 13 | Northern Aplomado Falcon | Arizona, Texas, New Mexico |
| 14 | Cape Sable Seaside Sparrow | Florida |

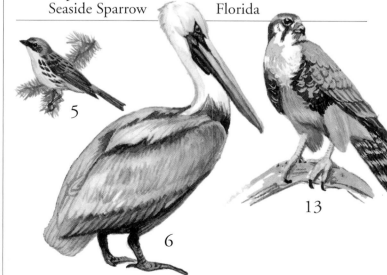

## You can help

All across the country people are working together to save endangered birds. Peregrine Falcons are being reintroduced, Piping Plover nests are being guarded on Maine's beaches and a captive breeding facility on Hawaii is working to save endangered Hawaiian forest bird species. You can be a friend to birds, too, and help make sure that no more species become endangered. Here's how.

- Make a bird feeder and remember to keep it full of food all winter long.

- Plant sunflowers, zinnias and other annual flowers in a garden or in pots. These plants produce lots of seeds and make great natural bird feeders in the winter.

- Build a birdhouse and put it up in early spring before the birds start nesting.

- Keep birds from crashing into a large window by making a black hawk silhouette from cardboard. Hang it outside the window.

- Make and sell birdhouses and bird feeders to raise money for conservation groups that protect birds and their habitats. Advertise your campaign in a local newspaper.

# Index